AF480081

Illustrations by Perri Hartenstein
Written by Alex Hartenstein
Edited by Erin O'Loughlin with special thanks to Stephen Tagle and Dan Ayer

Olivia
and the
Purple Whale

Illustrated by Perri Hartenstein   Written by Alex Hartenstein

Once upon a time, there lived a clever and imaginative girl named Olivia. Olivia loved computers, and she loved to make her own computer programs that did all sorts of wonderful things. Most of all, she loved making her friends happy. Making a computer program is a bit like doing a magic spell, but instead of magic words, you need code. Olivia was excellent at writing code!

When you make a magic potion, you need all sorts of ingredients, right? Well, when Olivia wrote code, she needed ingredients called functions. Each function could do one special thing. By mixing the functions in the right way, Olivia could create a computer program to do whatever she wanted.

One day Olivia was walking along the shore when she saw one of her friends.

"Hello Blue Whale!" she said.
"How are you today?"
"Hi Olivia!" said Blue Whale. Blue Whale had a wonderful sing-song voice and when she talked, her voice went high and low, and everything in between!

"I was thinking about my friend Octopus,"
continued Blue Whale.
"He invited me to a dinner party next week. He is always
showing off about how he can turn all different colors."

"Last time I was there, he said I was boring and blue."
Blue Whale sounded so sad that Olivia wanted to cheer her up.
"Blue is a great color for a Blue Whale to be," Olivia said.
"And you are wonderful, just as you are!"

Blue Whale thought a minute. "I like being blue a lot," she agreed.

"But I also want to know what it feels like to be different. "

"Just once, I'd like to be purple with spots too!"

Olivia thought hard. Was there a computer program that could help?
"I know how to do that!" she exclaimed suddenly.
"Do you remember my rainbow parrot program?"

"Last month, when Parrot had a rainbow party, I wrote a program with a function that turned all the parrots' feathers into bright rainbow colors."

"I could use the same function and put it in a whale-coloring program!"

"But Olivia, I am much bigger than a parrot," said Blue Whale sadly.
Olivia looked at her thoughtfully.
"First, I need a function to make you small enough to fit through the color-change function."

As she walked along the beach, Olivia thought about what functions she could write. But suddenly, she saw a function a few steps away, gleaming in the sand.

Running to it, she picked it up and threw the function into the air like a frisbee.
"Tell me your purpose!" she shouted. The function glowed.
"Hi there," it answered. "You can use me to make bubbles!"

Olivia grabbed her computer and began to type. As she typed, the function started spinning and spinning and big bubbles shot out in all directions.

Olivia laughed and slid the function frisbee into her backpack. "That will be useful when I take a bath," she said, but it won't help make Blue Whale smaller."

A little further on, Olivia saw another function. She threw it into the air and called out "Tell me your purpose!"
The function frisbee began to spin and stretch. It shouted, "Use me to make cats!"
Curious, Olivia picked up a pebble and tossed it through the function. Out jumped an orange cat!

Just then, she saw her friend Lola coming down the beach. Lola
also loved to write computer programs and she and Olivia often
shared their functions with each other.
"Hi Lola! I need your help. I'm looking for a function to make Blue
Whale smaller, so she can fit through my color change function.
I've found bubbles and cats, but nothing to change her size."
" I have the perfect function for you," said Lola happily.
"It controls the size of things! "

"Thank you!" Olivia said,
"Now what should I test it on?"
"Excuse me," meowed a voice.
Olivia looked down at the cat.
"I would like to be as big as a
house." she meowed.
"Can your function do that?"

Olivia threw the function frisbee into the
air and commanded, "Make this cat the
size of a house."

The function frisbee started to glow, basking the cat in a bright light.

The cat began to grow and grow and grow, until she was as big as a house!

"Meow! Thank you!" The cat boomed, and with a yowl, she jumped away and bounced a long the sandy shore.

Olivia was ready. Opening her computer, she thought about how
to mix the functions.
"First, the size changing function, to make Blue Whale smaller,"
she said, "Then, the color changing function, to make Blue Whale
purple with spots." She was about to finish, when she thought of
something. "I musn't forget to make Blue whale big again!" she
laughed, and added the size changing function again at the end.

"That's it, the program is ready! Blue Whale, where are you?" Olivia called. Blue Whale was singing nearby and rushed over to try it straight away. "Here goes!" Olivia shouted, and she pressed enter on her whale color changing program. The functions shook and whirred above Blue Whale. The first frisbee glowed, and sure enough, Blue Whale shrunk until she was the size of a parrot!

Next, Blue Whale was pulled through the color changing disc.
When she came out the other side, Olivia could see she was purple
with white spots! Finally, the first function made Blue Whale grow
back to her original size.

"How do you feel?" Olivia shouted. "Well..." Blue Whale swam in a circle. "I feel the same. But how do I look?" She couldn't see that she was a different color. "Olivia, I can't tell if I'm interesting!"

"Blue Whale, you're interesting whether you are blue or purple,"
Olivia smiled. "But you look very different. Let me show you!"
Olivia found the bubble making function in her backpack and
made a bubble. She sent it through the size changing function, and
the bubble grew one hundred times bigger.

"I'm purple with spots!" cried Blue Whale, looking at her reflection in the bubble. "Thank you Olivia. I'm sure Octopus will think I'm more interesting now!" She swam away happily.

That night at the dinner party, Octopus was dazzling in
a yellow striped suit.
When he saw Blue Whale, he rushed over.
"How fine you look!" he said.

"Won't you try the seaweed salad?" Look at my wonderful purple
whale!" Octopus cried to all the guests. He invited Blue Whale to
come to another party the very next week.

But when Blue Whale got home, she felt strangely sad. Octopus had seemed interested in Blue Whale's new color. But he still didn't seem very interested in her. Were they really friends? Or did Octopus only care about how she looked?

The next week, Blue Whale went to the dinner party, but first she asked Olivia to change her back to her normal blue color. "Oh, Blue Whale, you are looking dull!" Octopus said.

"You look wonderful Octopus," Blue Whale told him. "And I look wonderful too- whether I'm blue or purple with spots!" She swam away to find Olivia.

"It's fun to try new things," Blue Whale said to Olivia,
"And I'd like to use your computer program to try lots of other colors.
But real friends aren't worried about what you look like on the
outside."

Olivia and Lola agreed. "It's who you are on the inside that makes you a wonderful, interesting friend."

Behind the Scenes

Olivia and the Purple Whale is a story that can be used to teach a couple of important concepts related to calling functions.

Programmers write code using programming languages. The code that they write tells a computer, step-by-step, exactly what to do. Programmers often write thousands of lines of code - it gets very complicated!

To make long, complicated pieces of code more understandable, useful pieces of code are organized into smaller chunks called 'functions'. Ideally, each function is very short (say, only 5 lines of code). Each function must then be named. Programmers spend a lot of time thinking about how to name each function - ideally the name of a function should tell everybody exactly what the function does. In Purple Whale, there are four functions. Olivia could choose to name them: make_bubbles, turn_this_into_a_cat, change_parrot_color, and change_animal_size make_bubbles.

```
define make_bubbles():
       return lots_of_bubbles
```

Here we are just seeing the function definition - we aren't actually 'running' i.e. calling the function yet. We define the name of the function (in blue), and then in the parenthesis define what input arguments the function needs; in this case, there are no input arguments. When the function is called, it does something, and programmers say the function returns something, called the function output.

So : programmers first define functions, and then when they want to use them, they call the function; when called, the function can return output.

To call the function make_bubbles, Olivia would first have to define the function make_bubbles somewhere (or find it on the beach/internet!), and then to actually make the bubbles she would type this into her computer:

```
make_bubbles()
```

and bubbles would pop out of the function.

Other kinds of functions act on things, which in programming language means that they take input arguments. In order for the function to work, Olivia needs to give the function the actual arguments. In Purple Whale, the function that turns things into a cat is 'turn_this_into_a_cat(this)'. For Olivia to call the function (i.e. actually make it work), she says the name of the function and replaces 'this' with what she wants to turn into a cat.

So, Olivia types:

```
turn_this_into_a_cat(this="rock")
```

And out pops a cat!

Functions can take as many inputs as you want - programmers like Olivia just have to define what they need to make the function work. In Purple Whale we also see functions that take two input arguments. To call them, Olivia just needs to give the input arguments she wants. So :

```
change_animal_size(animal=cat, size= "as big as a house")
change_parrot_color(parrot=oliviasNeighbor, color= "rainbow")
```

At the end of the book, we see Olivia writing a new function that takes all the functions she found together. This shows how modular programming is! If we write good functions, we can always reuse them for new things whenever we need. Here's what Olivia's function could look like!

```
define make_whale_purple(whale):
    original_size = whale.size
    whale = change_animal_size(animal=whale, size = "as big as a
parrot")
    whale = change_parrot_color(animal=wh  ale, color = "purple with
white                        spots")
    whale = change_animal_size(animal=whale, size = original_size)
    return animal
```

And then to call the function she would say:

```
PurpleWhale = make_whale_pink(whale=BlueWhale)
```

If functions are well written, then it's a great idea to reuse them! Notice that the function 'change_parrot_color' wasn't a very reusable function - the name says it only works on parrots! Good thing that Olivia knows that that's just because of the size problem - the function only works on things as big as a parrot, otherwise they don't fit. The function 'make_whale_purple' is also not very reusable! It can only be used to make things "purple with white spots", and the name of it implies that it only works on whales! Olivia could write another function that can be used to change any animal to any color. It would look like this :

```
define change_animal_color(animal, color):
    original_size = animal.size
    animal = change_animal_size(animal=animal, size ="as big as a
    parrot")
    animal = change_parrot_color(animal=animal, color = color)
    animal = change_animal_size(animal=animal, size =
original_size)
    return animal
```
Every time Olivia wants to change the color of an animal, she could just reuse the 'change_animal_color' function! Other people could also use this function, so Olivia could share the function she writes. Programmers often share functions they write.

We see this in PurpleWhale, when Olivia finds functions laying in the sand - programmers find functions in 'open source' (publically available and shared) libraries on the internet, and can use them in their own code. Good programming is a lot about trying to make complex things as simple as possible, and it really feels like magic when things come together!

About the Sibling-Creators

Perri loves taking care of childrens' health and promoting their healthy development. She works as a pediatrician in Tucson, Arizona. She also loves art and illustrating . After learning that she could make art on her ipad anywhere and anytime she was hooked!

Alex loves learning, teaching and exploring the world. He works with data during the day in Berlin, Germany. While studying computer science he realized there were only 2 girls in a class of 100. One day while on a walk with his five year old niece, he started to tell the story of Olivia, a girl who could program magic!